BY DAN JENKINS

BUBBA TALKS

YOU GOTTA PLAY HURT

"YOU CALL IT SPORTS BUT I SAY IT'S A JUNGLE OUT THERE"

FAST COPY

FOOTBALL (with Walter Iooss, Jr.)

LIFE ITS OWNSELF

BAJA OKLAHOMA

LIMO (with Bud Shrake)

DEAD SOLID PERFECT

SEMI-TOUGH

SATURDAY'S AMERICA

THE DOGGED VICTIMS OF INEXORABLE FATE

THE BEST 18 GOLF HOLES IN AMERICA

DOUBLEDAY

NEW YORK • LONDON • TORONTO
SYDNEY • AUCKLAND

BUBBA TALKS

Of Life, Love, Sex,
Whiskey, Politics,
Foreigners, Teenagers,
Movies, Food, Football,
and Other Matters
That Occasionally
Concern Human Beings

DAN JENKINS

A MAIN STREET BOOK

PUBLISHED BY DOUBLEDAY

a division of Bantam Doubleday Dell Publishing Group, Inc.
1540 Broadway, New York, New York 10036

MAIN STREET BOOKS, DOUBLEDAY, and the portrayal of a building with a tree
are trademarks of Doubleday, a division of Bantam Doubleday Dell
Publishing Group, Inc.

Book Design by Cathy Braffet

Library of Congress Cataloging-in-Publication Data

Jenkins, Dan.
Bubba talks of life, love, sex, whiskey, politics, foreigners, teenagers,
movies, food, football, and other matters that occasionally concern human
beings / by Dan Jenkins. — 1st ed.
p.   cm.
1. Men—United States—Socail life and customs—Humor. I. Title.
PS3560.E48B8   1993
813'.54—dc20   93-15140
                                                          CIP

ISBN 0-385-47079-7

Printed in the United States of America

October 1993

First Edition

1 3 5 7 9 10 8 6 4 2

*This book is warmly dedicated
to all of my friends everywhere,
gentlemen and ladies alike,
who need to finish that drink
and go on home now.*

ACKNOWLEDGMENTS

THE AUTHOR WISHES TO EXPRESS HIS gratitude to all of the Bubbas and Bubba wives he knows for their help in the preparation of this book, although, of course, a good many of them may have contributed to it unknowingly.

On the following pages, over 130 subjects that are vital to the human experience are more or less arranged in the order in which Bubba himself might have thought them up while spending a reflective afternoon at Dottie's Paradise Lounge.

"WHO IS BUBBA?"

THE QUESTION IS USUALLY ASKED BY your effete Easterners and West Coast ponytails who pretend to like trout pizza and fat novels written by Ecuadorians.

Well, to start with, Bubba is *not* a Southern redneck who thinks a rented movie and a six-pack are quality entertainment.

That happens to be a distorted view of Bubba, a view largely advanced by people who can't appreciate the wisdom in a country song like "I Just Hope Those Honky-Tonks Don't Kill Me Before I Live Myself to Death."

Granted, there is more than one Bubba from Georgia who has spray-painted his girlfriend's name on an overpass, more than one Bubba from North Carolina who will list Jack Daniels among his 10 Most Admired People, and more than one Bubba from Texas whose wife's hairdo got caught in a ceiling fan.

But there is also more than one Bubba from Minneapolis who likes to do his Christmas shopping at Graceland, more than one Bubba from Chicago who has more appliances on his front porch than he does in his kitchen, and more than one Bubba from Rochester who has more curtains in his van than he has in his home.

The fact is, Bubba is an attitude more than anything—and there are sensible people who sleep better at night because they realize that without Bubba's attitude, biscuits and gravy might soon be run out of town by curried pumpkin soup, and then where would we be?

Bubba knows. We would all be so "politically correct," we would be marching in parades to protest battered lesbian seals, and eventually forced to refer to our halfbacks as African-American ball-carrier persons.

This is primarily why all of your Bubbas, no matter where they come from, choose to embrace the same philosophy of life, which is:

"There's always one more sumbitch than you counted on."

Part One

People Have Always Acted
Like That Whether You
Were There to Watch or Not

LIFE

BUBBA THINKS LIFE IS A PRETTY good deal, all in all, especially on those days when a man's got some money in his pocket and his Firebird has just come off the lube rack.

He knows it's a better deal for Americans than anybody else, of course. That's because your American has things to be interested in—football, cheeseburgers, adultery, pantyhose commercials— which keep him from wanting to make trouble like your foreigners do.

It's Bubba's guess that your trouble-making foreigners would enjoy life more if they didn't have to argue all the time about Buddha or Mohammed or whether Jesus went to Heights or Poly.

That's when they're not having to put up with earthquakes, tidal waves, volcanoes—that kind of thing.

It's too bad life treats foreigners this way, Bubba says, but better them than him.

One thing they might do is try eating fewer fishheads.

LOVE

A VERY DIFFICULT THING FOR Bubba to talk about, as it is for most normal men, he believes.

In fact, in all the years Bubba was married to Janie Ruth, he can't recall that he ever really opened up his heart on the subject, except for those afternoons he was with Vicki Lynn Kilgore at the Shady Valley Motel.

DEATH

IT'S ABOUT THE MOST INCONVE-
nient thing there is, and Bubba doesn't know
anybody who actually enjoys it, although the
Irish come close.

Bubba learned to handle the prospect of
death a little better after somebody told him about
reincarnation.

That got him to thinking about the life he
once had with Sophia Loren and looking forward
to his life with Priscilla Ann Thompson, the one who
got away in high school.

BABIES

BUBBA LIKES BABIES A LOT—AS long as there is somebody around to make them shut the fuck up.

He likes to pet a quiet little baby and watch it crawl around on the carpet and eat lint.

Everybody ought to like babies, he says, because if it weren't for babies, there wouldn't be mankind as we know it.

But babies should be left at home, Bubba believes. It truly amazes Bubba that you hardly ever see a baby in public that's not with a fat young mother and raising all kinds of hell because it obviously doesn't like nachos.

Bubba wishes more fat young mothers would either stop having babies or leave them in the Sears containers on the tops of their cars when they go inside the mall.

TODDLERS

IN BUBBA'S CONSIDERED OPINION, toddlers are more fun than babies, and, to a degree, less trouble.

For one thing, a toddler has practically become the same thing as a human being, and for another thing, a toddler is about to learn how to throw and catch a football.

Bubba would caution you not to turn your back on a toddler for very long, however. That's because a toddler's idea of a swell time is to try to pull off the ears or poke out the eyes of a Yorkshire terrier.

It's better all the way around, as Bubba sees it, if your dog is bigger than your toddler, and fairly nimble.

KIDS

A KID IS SOMETHING THAT FALLS in there somewhere between a pine knot and a teenager. Kids aren't old enough to wind up in jail yet, but they're old enough to get their butts whipped if they get caught shoplifting or damaging a neighbor's property.

Most of the time, Bubba always thought his own kids were sort of entertaining, even all those times when they broke their bunk beds, cracked the glass on the patio door, and set fire to their Barbies and G.I. Joes.

On the other hand, Bubba's first wife, Janie Ruth, didn't think her kids were all that amusing most of the time.

As she said to Bubba one night in a motherly tone of voice, "I just wish I could come home from work one goddamn time and not find a problem!"

TEENAGERS

OCCASIONALLY, IN MOMENTS OF extreme anger brought on by Bubba Junior and Janie Junior—the kind of anger where you kick your car to death because it has a flat—Bubba used to think the world would be a better place if all teenagers got sent off to maximum-security military schools and maximum-security convents when they turned fourteen.

He once made a list of the only things you would lose if this were the case.

1. MTV.
2. Fender dents.
3. Week-old pizza under the bed.
4. Treble.
5. A whole lot of back talk.

Almost everybody Bubba talked to about it seemed to like the idea.

TEENAGERS II

YOU COULD LET THE TEENAGERS out of those military schools and convents after about three years, at which point they would only have two things to say:

1. "You're a great guy, Dad—here's that money I borrowed last week."
2. "Mom, are you sure I can't run another errand for you?"

TEENAGERS III

BUBBA WAS A TEENAGER HIMSELF once, but he was a different kind of teenager.

He played football and was proud of it, and proud of all the limp-offs he caused—it helped build character.

His idea of a true American hero was John Wayne, who almost never played the electric guitar.

His car had a drink holder in it instead of a tape deck.

The songs he liked had tunes.

He danced The Two-Step and The Drag as opposed to The Disco-Fag Hop Around, which hadn't been invented yet by tone-deaf alien terrorists.

He only forgot his manners around barbecues.

And he respected anybody in a uniform, except for that sorry shitass over at the Conoco station.

WIVES

BUBBA IS STILL TRYING TO FIG-ure out what they want.

Bubba's good buddy Joe Ed Starkey, who's been married six times, keeps saying, "You can't do nothin' about 'em—they're flawed creatures."

Bubba is not that cynical. He keeps working at it. So far, he's pretty sure of this much:

They like to be hugged fairly often.

They like to get flowers.

They like to talk about shit.

The first two are easy enough. It's that last one that takes a lot out of you.

EX-WIVES

YOU CAN ACCUMULATE EX-WIVES real easy, Bubba says, particularly in this day of the no-fault divorce.

Among his friends, Bubba has noticed that you can get yourself an ex-wife if you refuse to spend any money on all that furniture she thinks you need to keep your house from looking like Beirut.

You can get an ex-wife if you keep on wanting to play golf on your vacation instead of going to Disney World.

You can get an ex-wife if you make that tragic mistake of not being able to recite poetry while you're trying to lift something heavy or fix the plumbing.

You can eventually get an ex-wife if you continue to give her anniversary presents that plug in.

The quickest way to get an ex-wife, of course, is to let Janie Ruth catch you with Vicki Lynn Kilgore.

Also, you can get a second ex-wife real quick if you let Vicki Lynn find some panties in your glove compartment that belong to Melissa Evans.

EX-WIVES II

THE SUBJECT OF EX-WIVES SEEMS to come up often when Bubba and Joe Ed Starkey and their pal Sidewall Thornton are drinking whiskey at Dottie's Paradise Lounge.

The other day they agreed that even though every story has two sides to it, there's never been a divorce in which the man didn't wind up as the shithead in the deal.

Sidewall said, "Boy, you can write that down in your diary. I still don't know what the problem was with Betty Sue."

Joe Ed chuckled, and said, "I said that to Rita one time. I said I didn't know what the problem was. She said, 'Well, that's the fuckin' problem right there.' I never said it to any of those others."

Sidewall still looked like he didn't understand.

That's when Bubba said it would all be explained in the Hereafter, he supposed, unless you wanted to go to Fort Worth and find out about it.

After a while Sidewall said it sure would be better on a man's health and golf game if he could somehow manage to stay on good terms with his ex-wives, but he guessed it wasn't possible unless they got married again and moved away to South Dakota—or Egypt.

Joe Ed said, "I used to start out trying to stay on good terms with 'em, but after you've been money-whipped as many times as I have, you tend to develop a bad attitude about it."

Sidewall said he heard not long ago, by the way, that his first wife, Denise, had passed away up in Oregon somewhere.

"That right?" Joe Ed said. "I never been lucky enough to have one die."

GIRLFRIENDS

IT'S BEEN BUBBA'S EXPERIENCE that your best girlfriends, those that last the longest, are the ones who are happily married to somebody else.

This is the girlfriend who lets you know up front that she's strictly in it for the adventure, like you are.

A girlfriend is not a mistress, incidentally. Your good mistresses are expensive to maintain, and Bubba would rather spend his money on a new set of Hogan irons.

Girlfriends are not always as good-looking as wives, but they're certainly more good-natured, which, by and large, is why they become girlfriends in the first place.

It's always a sad day, however, when the girlfriend suddenly turns out to be not so happily married and not so good-natured.

All you can do in this unfortunate moment, Bubba says, is heave a sigh, shake your head, and quietly say to yourself, "Oh, Christ—here we go."

GIRLFRIENDS II

ALL THINGS BEING EQUAL, Bubba believes you really ought to sort of try to avoid getting involved with a girlfriend who has just broken up with Conan Rambo.

Good as she may look, he may still be in love with her, and you just don't need that kind of problem.

BIMBOS

BIMBOS ARE NOT NECESSARILY hookers, at least not in the hard-core sense, but they can be just as dangerous nowadays. For all you know, they might have crawled through six sewers on their way to Dottie's Paradise Lounge or The Blue Note.

Not that Bubba and Joe Ed Starkey and Sidewall Thornton wouldn't treat themselves to a bimbo on occasion, purely for recreation, or maybe to take the pressure off.

Your bimbos can be very intriguing, like those two that Bubba met a month or so ago. They claimed to be sisters. Said their names were *Menage* and *Trois*.

Well, they were hard to resist, of course. But there's one thing Bubba and Joe Ed and Sidewall always do before they scoop a bimbo. They make sure she has her paperwork.

Sidewall even carries a penlight.

"Yeah, go ahead and laugh," Sidewall said the other night, "but old Cobalt Blue may save my life someday."

FEMALE BUBBAS

THEY LEAD A DOUBLE LIFE. You'll see the rascals around the office or somewhere downtown during the day, and they appear to be your dedicated, responsible secretary or receptionist, although one or two may give you a hint of what they're up to when they say something to you like "Where we gonna boogie tonight, ace?"

Then nighttime comes and they're out there on patrol in their skintight jeans, showing off their store-bought tits, chain-smoking Vantage 100s, drinking Bud Lites, discussing the size of Randy's dick, and saying fuck every other word.

Bubba's not fooled anymore. A lot of big talk is all they are.

RELATIVES

IT IS VERY HARD TO KEEP ALL OF your relatives straight when you only see them at funerals or sometime around Christmas.

Bubba still gets R.T. and Vermelle mixed up with V.G. and Wrenella. They're on his daddy's side, but R.T. and V.G. are both bald-headed and Vermelle and Wrenella never breathe, they just talk.

Bubba thinks Alma Lea and Milton are the ones who moved to Thorp Springs, but that could be Vineta and Cecil. Alma Lea collects figurines and Vineta frames her jigsaw puzzles, or it could be the other way around.

It could well be Milton who complains the most about diabetes, although Cecil has it, too.

Wilma and Mary Margaret are definitely sisters. One is married to Floyd and one is married to Doyle. Floyd and Doyle both like to stare at carpets.

Aunt Mozelle used to be able to keep it all straight, but she got mad about an antique lamp in somebody's will and hasn't spoken to anybody in the family for fifteen years.

SISTERS

BUBBA ONLY HAS ONE YOUNGER sister himself, so most of what he knows about sisters is what he's observed around Sidewall Thornton's house.

Sidewall has four—the fat one, the skinny one, the mean one, and the one who won't ever come out of the room that has the black window shades in it.

Basically, as near as Bubba can tell, your sisters seem to think they know more about everything than anybody, especially their own sisters.

BUBBA'S SISTER

BUBBA FEELS BAD ABOUT PATSY Claire and the hard life she leads, but he maintains his sister brought most of it on herself.

The old boy she fell in love with, A. C. Glasscock, did look a little like Elvis if you squinted at him and used your imagination, but Patsy Claire can't say Bubba didn't strongly advise her not to marry A.C. until he found a regular job and stopped dreaming about having his own fireworks stand someday.

That idea didn't rank high up on Bubba's list of your get-rich-quick schemes, frankly.

But she went on and married the hotshot, and now all she has to show for anything are those five screaming kids she has to take with her everywhere she goes, even when she drives by Buddy Robertson's Used Cars to see if A.C. is out there on the lot where he's supposed to be. He's been known to call in sick fairly often and go play paint ball.

Their wedding was a tip-off on what kind of future Patsy Claire had in store, if you want Bubba's opinion.

A.C. insisted on making the wedding arrangements, and one day he proudly announced that he had set it up at the famous South Fork Ranch down in Dallas—a special surprise for Patsy Claire.

Everybody got excited about this, even though the trip would be expensive and inconvenient.

Unfortunately, when everybody arrived in Dallas, they discovered the wedding wasn't at the South Fork Ranch, after all.

It was across J. R. Ewing Boulevard in a South Fork mobile home community, is where it was.

On top of that, nobody is likely to forget that it was right in the middle of the ceremony that A. C. Glasscock's mama blurted out, "Somebody kill that bug on the floor—it's gonna run up her dress!"

You could say it's been pretty much uphill for Patsy Claire ever since.

BROTHERS

BUBBA HAS OBSERVED THAT there are four kinds of brothers in the world, which anybody would know if they bothered to study it.

The older brother is a very serious person. He has just too darn many responsibilities at home and work to find anything remotely interesting about life. His wife has never heard or seen anything interesting, either. Certainly nothing worth smiling about.

The middle brother is a pure genius. He knows how to fake mental disorders and blackmail his folks out of free places to live and drug money.

The younger brother has big plans to be successful in business someday. He'll get around to doing something about it when he's thirty-five or forty and comes back from his latest ski trip.

The half-brother can often be a total surprise. You may not know he even exists until he shows up on your doorstep one day, wearing a bedsheet, high-top tennis shoes, and hair like Geronimo's. No, you don't have a spare room and you're not sure where he can find a job as an elephant trainer.

FATHERS

THE THING BUBBA REMEMBERS best about his daddy is how his daddy never talked to anybody in the family as much as he talked to the TV set.

This gave him something in common with most other daddies, actually.

Bubba's daddy would come home from work every night and sit in the same chair and eat his dinner off the same tray. It was from this vantage point that he could tell Ironside who the kidnapper was, or tell Kojak to watch out for that crazy sumbitch hiding in the closet with a knife.

Mostly, however, Bubba's daddy talked to news commentators and all of the vagrants and foreigners who turned up on the news every evening.

There was definitely a news broadcast on TV if Bubba overheard his daddy saying any of the following things:

1. "That's a crock."
2. "There's a liberal for you."
3. "I don't believe you can sell any of that crap in *this* house tonight."
4. "That's right. All of you lay down in the street now."
5. "Well, I've got a suggestion for *you,*

hoss. If you don't like it here, why don't you get your ass on over there to Mo-zambique?"

Bubba's daddy almost never saw anything good on the TV news.

Patsy Claire swears to this day that it was those I-raqis and I-ranians who caused his heart at-tack and killed him.

MOTHERS

GENERALLY, BUBBA SAYS, THEY fall into two categories.
Dark room, headache.
Sunny porch, no headache.

BUBBA'S MAMA

THEY DON'T MAKE WOMEN LIKE Bubba's mama anymore. If Bubba had to pin it down, he'd say they stopped about when the microwave oven came along.

There was never a household problem Bubba's mama couldn't handle with a smile. She cooked and cleaned and picked up and held down a part-time job all her life. She never got sick. As a matter of fact the only time she ever even had to lie down on the bed for a minute or two was when Florence died—she loved that Lab.

Bubba's mama was a great lady in all ways, and she left Bubba with a wonderful legacy, which was the recipe she invented for chicken fried bacon.

Dip pieces of bacon in milk.
Dredge in flour.
Sprinkle salt and pepper.
Place in cold skillet on hot stove.
Turn once.
Remove when brown.
Serve with Bisquick biscuits.

Bubba can still hear his mama's voice talking about her invention.

"The bacon don't shrink, and all the fat is preserved inside the crispy brown crunchy coating."

She was about half saint is all she was.

Part Two

Would You Rather Eat "Chef Timothy's Rare Duck Breast with Raspberry Tinge and Chestnut Purée," or Walk Barefooted Across Africa?

DOGS

TO BUBBA'S WAY OF THINKING, there aren't many things more entertaining than rolling around on the carpet with a slick-haired dog.

Dogs have many splendid virtues, he says.

1. They are entirely sympathetic about your problems at the office.
2. They enjoy hearing about your golf game, hole by hole, shot by shot.
3. They like the same TV programs you do.
4. Food will square most any differences you have with them.
5. They hardly ever object to anything on moral grounds.

NEWSPAPERS

AFTER ALL THESE YEARS, BUBBA says, you would think somebody might know how to put out a decent newspaper. Start with your average front page.

The top half is about a group of maniac foreigners who are throwing bombs at each other to see who can wind up with the most pairs of Gucci loafers and cable channels.

The bottom half tells you two things. It sheds new light on a tollbooth controversy that will obviously have a dire effect on mankind, and it brings you up-to-date on the city councilman who accidentally parked in a handicap zone and has hell to pay.

Nothing of interest on all those inside pages of the first section, unless you care about the storm that blew all the Taco Bells off Mombasa.

Nobody has ever read an editorial, it goes without saying, and the columns on that page across from the editorials don't matter to anybody who's not living in Israel.

Over in the business section, it's business as usual. The Dow and the prime and the deficit are deeply concerned that two and five-eighths may not equal one and three-fourths, although it's a good sign that four and one-third is more than three and two-fifths. Locally, your lessees and lessors are still at it.

Go to the lifestyle section and there's the old wood-carver again, sitting in front of her haunted house.

Bubba's not sure he would even subscribe to a daily paper if it weren't for the sports pages and TV log.

MAGAZINES

BUBBA PREFERS MAGAZINES THAT only deal with one subject.

You get what you pay for and know what to expect if the magazine is exclusively about football or golf or cars or guns or girls in garter belts.

Otherwise, you can't learn anything. All you do is wade through rock stars, painters, salads, castles, poverty, and a bunch of rich women trying on clothes.

BOOKS

IF A BOOK IS GOING TO HOLD Bubba's attention very long, it better be about Nazis or spies or private detectives, and fit in his pocket.

He's not good at remembering titles or the names of writers, but he seems to recall a few he liked.

1. *The Osterman Haldemans.*
2. *Code Name Hepatitis.*
3. *The Budapest Alpaca.*
4. *Lick the Blood Off My .38.*

Bubba stays clear of books that sound somewhat literary, such as *The Melancholy Dusk of Raymond Hoover,* or whatever it was called.

He's not big on two other kinds of books, either.

1. *Sensitive Women and the Withdrawn Jerks They Marry.*
2. *Wealth, Love, and Fame Before You Come Back from Lunch Next Tuesday.*

Bubba says thick books can be useful in the home, however. He once needed to fill up some shelf space, so he went to this secondhand book-store and bought himself a crate of those forty-pounders in assorted colors. Worked out real good.

TALK SHOWS

WHILE EVERYBODY'S BACK WAS turned, it seems, the best TV talk shows jumped from nighttime to daytime.

Bubba can't force himself to watch a talk show at night anymore. All you ever see, he says, is some actor telling the host about his new favorite disease. Or how he thinks America will find an important message in this movie he's just made about dead people who come back to life on a pirate ship and learn karate.

But daytime talk shows are something else. Only the other morning, Bubba was late for work because he couldn't tear himself away from the TV.

On Channel 3 there were these six teenage girls who had all dropped out of school and were living with fifty-five-year-old drywall workers who liked to carve the names of Oklahoma towns on their backs with Boy Scout knives. On Channel 5 there were these six housewives who had all dropped out of the PTA and joined biker gangs. And on Channel 9 there were these six couples who had all traded their babies for fishing boats.

It was a tough job for the old clicker.

MOVIES

BUBBA ENJOYS GOING TO THE movies. Mainly, he likes the ones where something happens.

One thing he's certain about, however. There can't be as many serial killers around as Hollywood would have you believe or there wouldn't be a pretty girl left in America.

Bubba has been known to sum up the various types of movies for his friends.

Romantic Movies

Edward doesn't see how he can divorce his wife as long as she's in the wheelchair. Rachel doesn't see how she can divorce her husband as long as he's off at war. Oh, well. Time to fuck again.

Cop Movies

"Make my day, Carlos, so I can hasta la vista your dope-crazed ass."

Adventure Movies

"Let me get this straight. We've only got twelve hours to get the diamonds out of the temple or the Nazi mummies will stick forks in our eyes?"

English Movies

They talked for three days and the girl never fell off the cliff.

Subtitle Movies

They smoked a lot, nobody could figure out how to stop the windshield wipers, and two or three people finally caught trains.

Western Movies

"A man's gotta do what a man's gotta do, Clarissa. Put the coffee on while I go kill the rest of those outlaws who forgot to shave today."

Science Fiction Movies

It doesn't seem possible that they can look, talk, and act just like humans when only three days ago they were in boxes of Cream of Wheat. "How can that be, Professor?"

Safari Movies

"He says he saw a white man here six weeks ago, but he thinks he went to Magoola Gomba with Ava Gardner."

Medical Movies

"I'm afraid the pain will slowly consume his whole body, but he probably won't go blind until there's no one left in the audience."

Historical Movies

That moat doesn't seem to do much good.

War Movies

"No, sir, I've never tried to land a B-17 before— I'm just a homespun tail-gunner from Pocatello, Idaho."

Horror Movies

"Is that you, Debbie?"

RADIO

"**O**MAHA, NEBRASKA, YOU'RE ON the air."

"Yes. Uh. Hello! Uh. I, uh, I'm retired after thirty-two years, you know? And, uh, I heard you talking about this AIDS deal. I have arthritis now. I have it in my shoulder and I have it in my arm. It's probably in my shoulder more than in my arm, and there are a lot of things about it. Of course, I'm one of the intelligent people who tries to keep up. Maybe you can go by me and maybe you can't, but what I mean is, we've got this government, you know? I mean, the government is up there in Washington and so forth, but the people, we're all out here with the passengers. I just think it's time somebody did something about it. That's my question."

MALLS

BUBBA NEVER MET A MALL HE didn't like. In terms of glamour and excitement, a mall represents the same thing to young people today that the big department store represented to Bubba in his youth.

But malls are a vast improvement.

A mall has foods of the world.

Malls are the country clubs of public golfers.

In a mall, you don't have to wait for an elevator to get to the Venetian blinds.

Malls are where you can find unbeatable low-price guarantees on most in-stock items.

Then there's the key thing, of course. Malls have more twats to look at.

GUNS

BUBBA WILL DEFEND ANYONE'S right to own a gun in this day and time, seeing as how the country is rapidly being overrun by your criminal element.

Even so, he doesn't think owning a gun should give you the right to shoot people because they honk their horns too loud.

You need to be a little more careful with guns than Sidewall Thornton was the night he was home cleaning three of his. Cleaning guns and drinking beer don't go together.

First time Sidewall accidentally shot himself, he didn't even feel it, he said. The second time it stung a little. It was the third time that he had to call an ambulance.

Bubba says it's also a good idea to keep guns out of the reach of children and most wives.

VCRS

HERE IS THE MOST AMAZING invention of Bubba's lifetime, but it's not as mysterious as most people think.

After the picture flies into the back of the TV set, it scampers up into the VCR. That's where the little Jap inside is organizing all of the colored dots while you stare at it.

It only takes a few seconds for the little Jap to make the dots start to hum. This means your VCR is working—don't worry about it.

There's supposed to be a way to tape one show while you're watching another one, but Bubba has tried everything and nothing happens.

He thinks it's probably a myth.

DEER HUNTING

BUBBA ENJOYS GOING DEER hunting once a year, but it's usually for the camaraderie because you hardly ever see a deer on Sidewall Thornton's lease.

Bubba knows one thing about it, though. Deer hunting is a little like the first time you sleep with a woman.

You've got your stalk, your chase, your excitement, you fire your shot—and then realize you've got a hell of a mess on your hands.

DOVE HUNTING

IT IS ESSENTIAL, BUBBA SAYS, that you and your friends go out and kill several hundred doves every year. This helps prevent the evil doves from taking over the entire western half of the United States.

But there is a right way and a wrong way to go dove hunting. The right way involves the following steps:

1. Store up enough whiskey and food for the weekend.
2. Make sure the bimbos can find the cabin.
3. When the bimbos find the cabin, tell the Mexicans to go kill the doves.

FISHING

FISHING CAN BE A PLEASANT thing to do occasionally, Bubba says, as long as you go for the scenery and the solitude and the beer.

Just don't expect any of Moby Dick's nephews to show up.

BOATS

THE CHARM OF OWNING A BOAT has always escaped Bubba. For one thing, you scrape it a lot more than you float in it.

You can't go out in the ocean in it. That's where the wind blows you into the Bermuda Triangle.

So you go up and down the Intracoastal and experience that big thrill of docking at Fay's Café & Bait Shop.

Bubba thinks boat owners ought to ask themselves this: If the oceans and lakes aren't shrinking, why are so many boats sitting in driveways?

ALCOHOL

PEOPLE WHO CIRCULATE THAT phony rumor about alcohol being a "depressant" are people who've never had enough to drink to turn into a matinee idol or a stand-up comedian or Mussolini.

Bubba and anybody else he would call a friend have always believed there's only one reason to drink, and that's to get drunk.

Bubba has made a thorough study of it and come to the conclusion that the best things to drink are Scotch, vodka, and beer. They'll take you the greatest distance.

Don't even think about gin unless you want to bang your head on something real quick.

Wine, of course, is the most deceptive thing of all. That's because a lot of people don't consider it drinking.

But you drink too much wine and you're even money to go off to kill the Clutter family.

THE BUBBA BURGER

THIS RATES EXTREMELY HIGH ON Bubba's list of pleasures, but you have to know how to cook it right.

Slap ground meat patty to a half-inch thick—that way you can eat two.

Sprinkle finely chopped onions on meat. Mash onions into meat with spatula.

Don't hold back on salt and pepper.

Drop in hot skillet covered with corn oil.

Mustard *and* mayonnaise on bottom of seedless bun.

Add hamburger dill chips.

Add slice of tomato that doesn't have a green knot in the center.

Add lettuce.

Place two slices of American cheese on meat while it cooks.

Put top of bun on cheese as it melts. Mash down on bun two or three times with spatula. Top of bun must shine.

Serve with Fritos, Bubba's favorite vegetable.

MUSIC

THE ONLY GOOD POPULAR SONG Bubba has heard in the past couple of years is "Get Yourself Some Alka-Seltzer and Feel Better Fast."

At least it has a tune.

Bubba has watched music slowly divide itself into two basic categories: (a) Decent Music (b) Insane Asylum Music.

Rock made sense when Creedence played it, but that was before all the singers yanked off their shirts, turned it into noise grenades, and went up in smoke.

Today, Bubba would rather count the cellos at a Mozart concert than try to listen to lunatics imitate musicians.

Rap poses a different question altogether. Are these songs or plea bargains?

COUNTRY MUSIC

OUNTRY MUSIC IS STILL RELI-able because it has melodies and plots and the occasional piece of advice.
Among Bubba's current favorites:

1. "If My Truck Was a Horse, I'd Shoot It."
2. "The Jukebox Lied Again."
3. "I Knew My Wife Had a Temper When She Made a Freight Train Take a Dirt Road."
4. "You Can't Rewind My Heart with Your Fast Forward Eyes."
5. "It's Somebody's Daughter, If You Stop to Think About It."

FOOTBALL

FEW THINGS IN THE WORLD ARE as important to Bubba as football. He likes both college football and pro football, although the college game is a more serious matter. From early September through the Super Bowl, Bubba goes into what Janie Ruth once described as his "football coma," which means he doesn't hear half of what is said to him, and often misunderstands the rest.

To be sure, Bubba has his favorite teams. He wears their sweatshirts and caps during the fall. Various neighbors claim to have seen him out in the carport on Saturday mornings, marching around in a circle to some of the fight songs he has on tape.

When big games come along, Bubba's generally good disposition is put to a severe test. How good a mood he's in over the next five days after a big college game depends entirely on whether his dedicated premed students and scholarly African-Americans have beaten your white trash and hired niggers.

GOLF

BUBBA TOOK UP GOLF LATE IN life but wishes he had started earlier. Not only would he be a better player now, he could have felt like a rich person all that time.

Seeing as how golf is a very difficult game to play well, Bubba says those times when you hit the ball squarely on the face of the club and watch it go in the general direction of where you aimed it can quite often fulfill your sexual needs.

The biggest problem with golf, he says, is trying to keep the ball from knowing who's swinging at it.

OPERA

SOMEBODY TRIED TO TELL BUBBA there is actually such a thing as an opera that has swordfights and whores in it.

Bubba doesn't believe that for a minute. If this was true, you couldn't get a ticket.

Joe Ed Starkey thinks they ought to make an opera out of his six marriages. There wouldn't be much singing, but there would be plenty of bathrobes and it would be loud enough.

Bubba can tell you one thing about opera singers, judging from those he's seen pictures of.

Those suckers can eat.

BALLET

BUBBA HAS NEVER BEEN TO A ballet, but he learned a crucial thing about it when he saw these ballet dancers on public television one night.

Most of your swans come up short on tits.

BASEBALL

IT WAS A BETTER GAME BEFORE A bunch of stupid owners started paying players 20 million dollars to tug at their balls for three or four hours a night, and never get a hit in the clutch.

BASKETBALL

BUBBA PREFERS THE COLLEGE game over the NBA—you don't have to worry about which movie star to root against.

THE OLYMPICS

THEY JUST AREN'T THE SAME FOR Bubba without Russia to hate. But he has some ideas about how to make a few of those abnormal events more interesting.

Let all of the ski racers come down the mountain at the same time.

Put more mud puddles on the other side of more hurdles.

If the pole vaulter doesn't clear the bar, he comes down in a vat of maple syrup.

Give the big husky fellows more than three tries to spin around and sling the Olympia Dukakis out of the stadium.

Take the bobsled out of that trough. Put fraternity boys in the bobsled with a keg of beer. Point the bobsled downhill toward a busy intersection.

Eliminate Sitting Around as a decathlon event.

Synchronized Swimming is a tough one. Maybe throw a toaster in the pool.

CARS

BUBBA DOESN'T UNDERSTAND why anybody would buy a new car. A new car is a used car the minute you drive it off the lot.

There are plenty of perfectly good used cars around that will get you there and back, that are clean, that are "fully loaded," as they say, and won't die on you in traffic because the digitals are having an argument with each other.

Also, Bubba is somewhat partial to makes and models he can spell.

CAR RACING

AS A SPORT OR A PASTIME OR A way of life, Bubba is not as intrigued with car racing as he once was. In fact, he has about half decided that it's been a terrible influence on American motorists.

Seems like every sumbitch on I-95 these days wants to tailgate you or cut your ass off, thinking he's some kind of Richard Petty.

It grieves Bubba to say so, but he believes you can lay the blame for this state of affairs directly on Daytona's doorstep.

"PRESSURE COOKERS"

TIME WAS, BUBBA RECALLS, when a man eagerly looked forward to driving out on the highway and devoting part of his workday to hanging around The It'll Do, or some other convivial establishment where housewives go to seek thrills.

Pressure cookers fill a need, of course. They sprang up several years ago, as you may know, when various entrepreneurs discovered that there are these thousands of restless wives and mothers in America who yearn for something to do in those dull, humdrum hours between breakfast and dinner.

The entrepreneurs went out and rented vacant warehouses and put bars and music in them. Thus, the restless wives and mothers had somewhere to go to meet new friends after fixing breakfast and getting Dad and the kids off to work and school—and before having to rush home in time to take the roast and potatoes out of the pressure cooker and stick dinner in the oven.

Bubba had many memorable good times at pressure cookers, but somehow the charm wore off, he says, when he dropped by The It'll Do around 10:30 one morning and found Janie Ruth dancing with Booger Red Brannon.

Part Three

Never Let On That You Hate
Something a Lot or They'll
Start Making More of It

WORK

BUBBA BELIEVES IN HARD WORK. If you work hard at your job, you'll get ahead. Of course, if you want to go any higher, you'll have to kiss some ass.

That's how businesses are run. Business set it up this way sometime after the Industrial Revolution.

Bubba has been a salesman all his life. Right now, he sells big ones and little ones. If he sells little ones, he has to sell about five thousand of them a year to come out all right. If he sells big ones, he only has to sell two.

Bubba is proud of being a salesman. He says everybody in the world is a salesman of one kind or another. It doesn't matter whether you deal in floor covering or paint Hindus in flower beds, you're a salesman.

BOSSES

MAYBE IT'S JUST BEEN COIN-
cidence, but Bubba has always seemed
to work for a phony sumbitch who refers
to himself in third person, the way C. E. Latson does
today.

When C.E. is talking to people in the office,
he says:

"C. E. Latson knows what it takes to make
this company run the way it's supposed to. C. E.
Latson doesn't have time for coffee breaks. C. E.
Latson would like to spend more time with his kids,
but he's busy keeping this office in order. Ask C. E.
Latson a question about this company and he has
the answer. C. E. Latson knows what it takes to be
a winner. That's what you better not forget about
C. E. Latson."

What Bubba's boss doesn't realize is that
he's known around the office behind his back as
"E. C. Lapper."

His secretary, Julie Bob Grant, started it and
it seemed to catch on.

CLOTHES

YOU NORMALLY FIND BUBBA IN a white shirt and jeans or khakis, and boots, sneakers, or loafers. He has a dark sport coat that's good for special occasions—births, deaths, Thanksgiving dinners, reunions.

Vicki Lynn gave Bubba a crewneck sweater for Christmas once, but he never wore it again after Sidewall Thornton saw him in it and said to him in a sissy voice, "Hey, there, Cookie Baby."

WOMEN'S CLOTHES

WOMEN OBVIOUSLY DON'T want to dress for men, Bubba says. If they did, they would all wear short skirts slit up the side, high-heel ankle-strap shoes, hose with seams up the back, and low-cut blouses.

HARDWARE STORES

"**I** DON'T KNOW WHAT YOU CALL it, but have you got one of those things that's about this long and has a deal that curves around and looks kind of like—well, it looks a little like *that*, I think—except it's supposed to be bigger, with a knob or something on top, and a wooden handle, and there's a thing you ought to be able to pull *up* with, you know, in case you're trying to . . . I'll tell you what. Just forget it. I'm gonna have to go back home and see what the fuck she's talking about."

COMPUTERS

PEOPLE WHO THINK THERE'S something magic about computers haven't given it as much thought as Bubba.

See, there's this World Computer Center over there in Japan. It's got about 20 million little chinks working in it twenty-four hours a day. They're busy every minute, thumbing through dictionaries and dealing with arithmetic problems.

If the little chinks didn't stay on top of everything so they can answer all the questions that come in, that computer in Joe Ed Starkey's office would be useless.

WELFARE

BUBBA ARGUES THAT YOU'LL never get an accurate total of how many people are on welfare until you count the United States Senate, the House of Representatives, every bureaucrat in federal and state government, and those ten old boys in hard hats on every city street who stand around and eat donuts and watch the guy with the jackhammer.

INSURANCE

YOU WANT TO TALK ABOUT your slick old boys, Bubba says. Insurance is the biggest con game ever perpetrated on the American people.

The only insurance Bubba has is what's required by law, and the only reason it's required by law is because insurance companies provide free blowjobs for politicians.

The great majority of insurance companies have never paid anybody a dime for any loss. The rest only pay a fraction of what something is worth if it gets stolen, burned down, flooded, or blown away by one of those tornadoes that goes crazy and veers out of Kansas.

It's all in the fine print on your policy, which nobody reads until the loss occurs. Right there on Page 16 it says you didn't suffer any loss unless it happened between 2:37 and 3:08 in the afternoon on Feb. 11 while Tony Bennett was singing on the radio.

This is why you see all those tall insurance buildings in every city. You'd think they wouldn't flaunt it.

POLITICS

BUBBA BELIEVES STRONGLY IN exercising the right to vote, but he has hard and fast rules about the candidates and issues that will get his vote.

1. Never vote to expand or extend anything because it will raise your taxes more than they will be raised ordinarily.
2. Never vote on any kind of environmental issue because *yes* may mean *no* or *no* may mean *yes*—the bird-watchers will trick you any way they can.
3. Always vote against the incumbent unless he's one of your golfing buddies.
4. Never vote for a lawyer, naturally.
5. Never vote for a hairpiece.
6. Never vote for a shiny suit.
7. Never vote for a pair of tasseled loafers.
8. Never vote for a man under five feet four.
9. Never vote for anybody from Massachusetts.
10. Never vote for any man or woman who has a relative in the ready-mix concrete business.

ABORTION

BUBBA CAN'T UNDERSTAND WHY this is a complicated issue for anybody, or why it makes people yell and cuss and throw themselves in front of moving vehicles.

It is very simple.

Abortion is wrong and should be against the law for everybody but your own daughter.

SEXUAL HARASSMENT

BUBBA IS ALL FOR DOING WHATever it takes to put an end to sexual harassment. It is a disgusting thing, he says, and he knows what he's talking about because he has been a victim of it himself on more than one occasion.

He vividly remembers that night when Maxine Shaw rubbed up against him at The Blue Note and said:

"I want to fuck you, Bubba. If you fuck me, I won't tell your wife. If you don't fuck me, I'll tell your wife you did."

Bubba vows to fight on the side of feminists to destroy this dreaded epidemic.

POLITICAL CORRECTNESS

BUBBA WAS IN DOTTIE'S PARA-dise Lounge the night this young fellow in a three-piece suit came in and ordered a "cola."

Dottie was behind the bar and asked what kind of "cola" the young fellow wanted.

He said, "Any kind will do. It wouldn't be politically correct for me to mention a brand."

Dottie was polite enough to take the Marlboro out of her mouth before she called him an asshole.

Bubba decided to study up on this "political correctness" thing. He found some stuff in a newspaper that he took back to Dottie's on another night in order to educate Joe Ed and Sidewall on the issue.

Near as Bubba could figure, everybody was now supposed to be in favor of "diversity" when it comes to having "multiculturalism" in government so there can be "race-specific remedies" to cure the "disparate impacts" on society's "heavily gendered nature."

Sidewall said no problem. Long as it didn't affect a man getting any pussy.

AIR TRAVEL

WHAT HAS HAPPENED TO AIR travel lately is a terrible shame, Bubba says.

It used to be a pleasant experience. No flight was ever crowded, you could smoke, and you had all these pretty young girls to bring you whiskey and food.

Now you've got boys and old women for stewardesses telling you they're all out of the chicken. Worse, you're crammed in there with all those businessmen who carry on four hanger bags and two briefcases each, mothers with steamer trunks and screeching kids, and an assortment of giant hairballs in tank tops, swimsuits, and sandals.

If there were truth in advertising, Bubba says, they would call it Flying Pig Pen.

SPACE TRAVEL

BUBBA IS ALL IN FAVOR OF space travel—they may find a cure for the common cold up there on one of those Plutos someday.

What he can't understand, however, is why it has to cost taxpayers thirty million dollars to figure out a way for an astronaut to take a shit.

HOTELS

BUBBA HAS ALWAYS HAD A JOB that requires travel now and then, so he's become an authority on what a good hotel should have to offer.

1. Room with cable TV.
2. All-night coffee shop or twenty-four-hour room service.
3. Gift shop that stays open late and sells cigarettes, papers, magazines, and toothpaste.
4. Patty sausage on the breakfast menu.
5. No trainees behind the front desk.
6. No live music in the bar.
7. Food available in the bar.
8. Bartender doesn't know any jokes.
9. Baptist convention is across town.
10. Parking attendant speaks English.

WEATHER

UNLESS HE WANTS TO PLAY golf, Bubba's favorite days are those when it's dark, dreary, cold, and raining, sleeting, or snowing outdoors.

On days such as this, absolutely nothing whatever is expected of Bubba, least of all an errand to run or a customer to call on.

It's an opportunity for Bubba to sit by a window in a diner or at Dottie's and drink coffee or beer, visit with friends who come and go, collect his thoughts, and look outside occasionally to watch humanity deal with itself.

Bubba says people who don't know how to take advantage of dark, dreary, cold days will be dead of hyperactivity or undue worry by the time they're fifty-seven.

HAIRCUTS

BUBBA STILL GOES TO JIMMY Ray to get his hair trimmed. Jimmy Ray only charges eleven dollars and has Bubba out of there in fifteen minutes. Another good thing about Jimmy Ray is, he doesn't know anything to talk about.

Bubba has never understood why some of his friends choose to patronize those fancy joints that all have names like "Hair Today, Gone Tomorrow."

Go in a joint with a name like that, you waste two hours, it costs thirty-five dollars, and you get Dracula for a barber.

BANKS

BUBBA FINDS IT A CURIOUS thing that bankers are allowed to steal your money without being called criminals.

Give a bank your paycheck but it doesn't get credited to your account until the bank is able to charge you so much for overdrafts that your paycheck is only worth half of what you deposited.

But this isn't known as theft, it's known as sound banking practice.

Meanwhile, your banker will only loan money to a rich man to buy himself a bigger yacht.

Your average citizen goes in to borrow money because he has a great idea, but the banker either laughs at him or gets mad.

"See, I would put them everywhere in the country. You'd drive your car up to a window and pick up the fast food. They would be easy to find because of the golden arch."

"Sir, you have one minute to leave this office or I'm calling the police."

STRESS

STRESS RESULTS FROM STAYING pissed off too long.

Bubba and Joe Ed Starkey believe that getting drunk or kicking inanimate objects are still the best ways to relieve stress, or pissed-offness, if you will.

Sidewall Thornton has a different idea. Sidewall recommends farting in public.

Sidewall likes to fart at the 7-Eleven while the Haitian is ringing up his beer and lottery tickets. He says farting loud and long in crowds often helps him integrate back into society when he's feeling separate and tense and confused.

Several people have learned the hard way never to pull Sidewall's finger if he asks them to do it in the middle of a social gathering.

DINNER PARTIES

ONE OF THE CRITICAL THINGS about a dinner party is where you happen to be seated, Bubba has learned from experience.

You don't want to be next to Corinne Conklin unless you're vitally interested in her daughter's wedding plans.

You don't want to be next to E. D. Weatherly, who believes somebody could write a very funny book about his twenty-seven years with Southwestern Bell.

You don't want to be next to Norris Gaddy, who took care of a real interesting customer last week at Allied Discount Tires. In due time, Norris will think of something interesting the customer said.

At all costs, you don't want to be next to Rowena Botts, an expert on curtains and drapes who somehow manages to tie this in with her dental history.

Frankly, there is no good seat at a dinner party. Aside from the grinding small talk, the hostess is a cinch to serve food that most men have never seen before in their whole lives.

Smart money makes an excuse to leave early and go get something to eat.

PRENUPTIAL AGREEMENTS

LIKE MOST PEOPLE, BUBBA HAD always assumed your prenuptial agreement was a financial document that rich folks thought up to protect themselves from each other, but then he heard somewhere that this isn't necessarily the case.

Evidently, there are couples around who like to put down on paper how they intend to live their lives after they get married.

Bubba passed this news along to Joe Ed Starkey one night at Dottie's.

Joe Ed said, "Hell, I missed the boat. I should have said I hereby state I intend to chase women, stay drunk half the time, and spend most of my money on golf. Sign here, Rita."

REUNIONS

YOUR FIRST HIGH SCHOOL RE-
union is a landmark occasion in your life
because you never quite recover from the
shock of seeing so many foxes that have turned into
hogs, or so many hogs that have turned into foxes.

The star of the night at Bubba's high school
reunion—and Sidewall and Joe Ed agreed on it—
was Edna Lou Cheatham. She was such a scag in
high school, her nickname was "Parachute," as in
"Hit the silk, Edna."

But Edna Lou had somehow taken rich over
the years and had been rebuilt from the ground up.
She seemed to enjoy causing all that whiplash in
her triumphant return.

Bubba wasn't surprised that all of his ex-
wives were in attendance, mainly to prove they had
kept their shape and didn't need to dye their hair
yet.

Janie Ruth came with her new husband, T. R.
Simms. Vicki Lynn came with her new husband, Lo-
gan Whatley. Melissa came with her new husband, Crocodile Minyard.

Bubba and Joe Ed and Sidewall took the
precaution of not taking dates to the reunion in order to see what might develop if a few stones were
overturned.

This was lucky for Bubba. Priscilla Ann Thompson flew in from Houston without her husband, and Bubba danced with her off and on throughout the evening.

Priscilla Ann mentioned that she might be moving back home after her divorce was final, and Bubba whispered to her that he might be in love for the first time in his life.

Hitler was at the reunion, a man otherwise known as Coach Teague.

Coach Teague only acknowledged Bubba and Joe Ed and Sidewall once all night long. That was when he walked past the three of them at the bar, shook his head sadly, and said, "There's the boodle boys."

PHILOSOPHY

BUBBA BELIEVES YOU CAN FIND more useful philosophy on the signs behind a bar than you will in some book that was written by a goatee in the Balkans.

Among his favorites that have adorned the walls of Dottie's Paradise Lounge:

THERE IS NO SUBSTITUTE FOR A LACK OF PREPARATION.

THE OTHER LINE MOVES FASTER TILL YOU GET IN IT.

NOSTALGIA IS NOT WHAT IT USED TO BE.

TRUTH IS ONE OF MAN'S MANY OPTIONS.

FRIENDS THAT COME AND GO NEVER LEAVE QUICK ENOUGH.

IF YOU CAN SMILE WHEN THINGS GO WRONG, YOU HAVE SOMEBODY IN MIND TO BLAME.

SUICIDE WILL END MOST ARGUMENTS, EXCEPT IN THE HOME.

TRIVIA GAMES

BUBBA AND HIS FRIENDS STILL play trivia games at the bar in Dottie's Paradise Lounge. There was a night only last week when a few questions made the rounds.

Bubba: "Who were the Four Horsemen at Notre Dame?"

Sidewall: "Grange, Thorpe, Gipp . . . Rockne."

Joe Ed: "Who succeeded Winston Churchill as Prime Minister of England?"

Bubba: "Alistair Cooke."

Sidewall: "Who was Hubert Humphrey's running mate in 1968?"

Joe Ed: "Sergeant York."

Bubba: "What year did the Tet offensive start?"

Sidewall: "Jane Fonda."

Joe Ed: "Who were the eight original astronauts?"

Bubba: "Shepherd, Glenn, Carpenter . . . Seale, Hoffman, Hayden, Cleaver . . . Yeager."

They all agree that trivia games aren't what they used to be. Too easy.

JEWISH BUBBAS

BUBBA HAS A FEW FRIENDS, HE would classify as Jewish Bubbas. None of them, as it happens, wear those little skullcaps.

Al Levine builds shopping strips, keeps bimbos stashed in secret apartments, and likes to refer to himself as "Big Dick Levine." He goes to Vegas four times a year.

Stack 'Em Up Sam is the developer who knows how to put 250 condos on only 5 acres of swamp. He tells short jokes about tall black people and sometimes handles his cigar like Groucho Marx when the duck fell out of the sky.

Radio Free Larry thinks he knows everything about sports and calls famous athletes by their first names—Michael, Nolan, Emmitt, Troy, Thurman. He wears grimy jeans, seldom shaves, seems to be in a new business every six months, and wishes he were from Georgia.

Trader Benny is a good guy even though he did six months in a federal joint for what he described as "a problem with mathematics that was too complicated for the government to understand completely."

Bubba has a lot of fun with these Jewish Bubbas but he still gets their holidays mixed up because their holidays sound like fish and musical instruments.

That's why he always has to say to Big Dick Levine or Radio Free Larry, "Tell me again when your bowl games are."

HEALTH

WITH A CERTAIN AMOUNT OF diligence, Bubba goes over a checklist to make sure he's healthy.

1. Does he still have a good appetite?
2. Can he cough it up?
3. Can he spit it out?
4. Can he put on both socks without straining a back muscle?
5. How bad did it hurt when he took a piss this morning?

DOCTORS

DOCTORS ARE LARGELY IN THE business of killing people, Bubba thinks.
They figure the more they can thin out the population, the easier it is to get starting times on golf courses.

DENTISTS

"**I** KNOW YOU ONLY CAME IN FOR a filling but let me show you what I've found on your X ray. See this line? That's your San Andreas Fault. When it goes, which could be any minute, the whole left side of your face will fall off. Nothing we can't deal with, however. I think eight lower implants and total upper dentures should do it. You'll be out of here in less than ten months, and it shouldn't cost more than, oh, twenty-five thousand dollars—ballpark."

ILLNESS

MOST PEOPLE AREN'T SICK. They just want to act like they are. It gives them something to talk about.

Bubba says if you want to watch two or three hundred people get well quick and scatter, walk in the waiting room at a clinic and holler, "Two for one at Pic N' Save!"

DRUGS

LIKE ANY TYPICAL AMERICAN male, Bubba went through his drug periods.

He smoked weed when it was supposed to be the thing to do. Finally gave it up for two reasons. One, he got tired of staring at Chinese hospitals, which other people called office buildings. Two, he got tired of never knowing exactly what the topic was in any conversation.

He took his share of speed during the pill-popping era. That got to be inconvenient—all those times he urgently drove to Arizona and back and never remembered why he went in the first place.

Cocaine made him brilliant for a while. Then he discovered that it stole most of his hard-ons and left him with nothing but huge bar tabs and all those inaugural addresses he could deliver on the spur of the moment.

Bubba enjoys telling war stories, of course, but he's been a happier and healthier man ever since he went back to whiskey only.

DREAMS

BUBBA WAS RELIEVED TO LEARN on TV one day that it's normal to have sexual dreams.

For weeks he had been having the same dream about being the only judge in a bikini contest when all of the girls suddenly turned into nymphomaniacs and slung him down on a gigantic mattress.

Sidewall said, "You talking about a dream or a Mexican border town?"

Sometimes, Bubba's sex dreams can turn into nightmares.

Like the one where he's Robin Hood and these Dallas Cowboy cheerleaders come out of the forest and strip naked but can't get his tights off.

CONDOMS

CONDOMS ARE FOR QUEERS. Bubba staunchly believes that his wholesome sperm deserves to enjoy its freedom and he likes to think it has a grin on its face while it's splashing around in the lagoon or playing softball or trying on caps.

GOD

THERE IS NO QUESTION THAT God is an American. God may have started out in Europe but he came to America as soon as he noticed that we were basically good-hearted people who bathed regularly and would someday invent central air-conditioning.

Bubba says people who sometimes have doubts about God being an American just need to remind themselves of where cold meatloaf sandwiches and college football came from.

Bubba loves God and tries to go to church every Easter. He also prays to God in his own quiet way, usually in those moments when he would dearly like to put a tee shot in the fairway on a long Par-4 or badly needs a touchdown in the fourth quarter.

But he understands completely that there will be those occasions when God is in Palm Springs with his phone off the hook.

Part Four

Intelligent People Would Be As Smart As They Think They Are If They Had Better Sense

HISTORY

IT FRUSTRATES BUBBA THAT YOUNG people today don't seem to have much interest in any history that wasn't on TV. It's like if the history didn't happen on TV, they only have your word for it, and what good is that?

Bubba's own kids used to complain about history being so boring. They didn't care what year the Vietcong bombed Pearl Harbor, or about any of that stuff where the Jewish people climbed over the Palestine Wall in Berlin and bought an island from somebody in the Bible so they could start Israel.

They did know that John Brown shot Abraham Lincoln in a picture show, and that somebody was President for twenty-five or twenty-six years one time. The old boy in the wheelchair.

EDUCATION

TEACHERS ARE THE MAIN REASON
so many people are uneducated, Bubba believes. Teachers are absolute masters at making any subject seem dull. Students nod off, cheat
on exams later, nobody learns anything.

Just off the top of his head, Bubba can think
of three examples of how teachers go about this:

Group Sex

"The house where they would meet was built in
1928. It was a large two-story Tudor Revival. It had
a sandstone chimney and a gabled porte cochere
that extended north. The wallpaper in the living
room . . ."

Telephone Sex

"Alexander Graham Bell was born in Scotland, and by the age of three . . ."

Oriental Sex

"The Ming Dynasty . . ."

WARS

IF YOU GO BACK A WAYS, BUBBA says, most wars were fought by people in funny hats.

If you come forward a little, most wars were fought because generals wanted to write books about it later.

THE CIVIL WAR

YOU HAVE TO READ BETWEEN the lines of all the textbooks to know why the Civil War started and why it was fought, Bubba says. You also have to keep in mind that the textbooks were written by Yale and Princeton, which was part of the payday when the North won.

The Civil War wasn't about slavery, that's obvious. It wasn't about a New York conglomerate wanting to change the name of Manassas to Bull Run. And it had nothing to do with a bunch of wild Southern boys itching to jump their horses over every hedge in Pennsylvania because Scarlett O'Hara hinted they might get laid if they came back as heroes.

It was about real estate. Northerners were fed up with fighting bad colds half the time. They wanted to take over the South so they could build winter resorts and enjoy the South's year-round golf courses.

That's why Northerners actually instigated the war. They knew if they bad-mouthed the South enough, the South wouldn't be able to take it any longer. The North knew that one day either Stonewall Jackson or Jeb Stuart would say to Robert E. Lee, "That's it, Bobby—let's go."

Not that it wasn't an overall good thing for the North to win.

It would seem kind of strange, even a little goofy, for the Washington Redskins to play their home games in Montgomery, Alabama.

WORLD WAR I

DON'T HAND BUBBA ANY OF that archduke business. One less little clown of an archduke in the world wouldn't have mattered to anybody.

The Kaiser wanted France, that's all. They never should have taken him to the Folies Bergere one night.

WORLD WAR II

BOY, THERE WAS A COCAINE deal for you, Bubba says. No way old Adolf could have made all those psycho speeches on his own.

Any doubts about cocaine being responsible for World War II were removed the day Hitler suddenly leapt out of his chair and screamed, "Russia? Why not??"

WORLD WAR III

IT MIGHT NOT HAVE EVER STARTED if Vicki Lynn hadn't made Bubba put on a coat and tie and go to dinner at one of those no-smoking, wine-only joints. The Crocheted Zebra. Something like that.

Stanislav brought the menu and right there on the first page was a brief note from Chef Timothy informing Bubba and the other customers that they were total morons about food.

Then came the choice of only two soups, either curried pumpkin or pear-roquefort.

"Pasadena," Bubba said, nicely.

Bubba ordered a main course that was apparently named after a bullfighter. It came with carrots carved into little flowers and some long green beans that were cooked almost as tender as swizzle sticks.

His thin slice of veal was swimming around in a pool of blood with miniature football helmets for company.

Bubba said to Vicki Lynn, finally, "You can't find a deal like this just anywhere. It won't cost more than $125 tonight to not smoke, not drink, and not eat."

Vicki Lynn said, "You just won't ever try to acquire any suave, will you?"

"I've got plenty of suave," Bubba said. "It's right here. Timothy poured it all over my fucking meat."

That was only the start of it, of course. It went on from there, several hours into the night after they got back home. Numerous past sins were remembered and debated.

It was in the heat of battle that Bubba quoted his buddy.

He said, "I'll tell you one thing, Vicki Lynn. You're living proof of what Sidewall says—'Single girls are the friends of fun, wives are the enemies of happiness.'"

She glared at Bubba and asked him to repeat that. He made the mistake of doing it.

"I see," she said. "Well, he always was a *deep* motherfucker!"

That was when a few household items began to get broken.

Bubba signed the divorce papers about ten days later.

He celebrated by cooking himself a pot of beans.

BUBBA'S CAN'T-MISS BEANS

DUMP A BAG OF NAVY BEANS or pintos into large pot. Soak in hot water for a while. They don't have to soak overnight like your grandmother once said.

Chop big white onion into blocks and throw in.

Add finely chopped garlic.

Two or three drops of Tabasco.

Cover whole surface of water with black pepper.

Salt to your taste. You can do more later.

Slice up pound of Oscar Mayer center cut bacon in one-inch chunks and fry slowly in big black iron skillet.

When bacon looks crispy-chewy brown, pour everything into pot, including the flavory grease. Don't waste a drop.

Add a little more hot water. Add a little more pepper.

Bring pot to gurgling boil, then cook on low for two and a half hours.

Remove lid of pot only once, halfway through, to see if hot water needed.

Serve with Premium crackers because you don't know how to make cornbread.

EUROPE

BUBBA SAVED UP AND WENT ON this package tour of Europe a few years ago to see what it was all about. It was mostly about trying to ditch the tour guide and stay out of cathedrals but not miss the bus.

He was glad he satisfied his curiosity about Europe, though, and had a number of things to report to Joe Ed and Sidewall.

1. Switzerland was the tallest.
2. Your Englishman doesn't seem to mind finding a bullet in his meat.
3. France doesn't care if you sit in a sidewalk café all day.
4. Italy won best ruins.
5. Your Germans act like they're about half ready to try it again.

SOUTH AMERICA

FROM WHAT BUBBA'S HEARD, there's not much to do down there but over-throw governments and tap-dance around scorpions.

HAWAII

HAWAII IS JUST ABOUT THE most exotic place Bubba has ever been, tropical-wise.

He hopes there will be another convention out there someday.

He was sorry he didn't see any Hawaiians —he was told he would have to go to Tahiti to do that.

But his hotel was right on the ocean. He liked watching the surfers trying to stand up on their big bars of soap, and he liked eating those platters of hookie nockies and drinking those tall neekie cockies.

CANADA

BUBBA HAS A QUESTION FOR Canada. How do you like being Canada? There you sit. Right up there. Bigger than a pregnant Montana. But nobody in the United States gives a damn or ever thinks about you.

There was a rumor one time of a Northwest Mounted Policeman who didn't have an inferiority complex, but nobody bothered to track it down.

IRELAND

HOW ABOUT THAT CLUSTER OF fun-loving intellectuals? It bewilders Bubba that they can't think up something better to do after a hundred years but kill each other over religion and jobs with the sanitation department.

Well, it keeps the nuns hopping on the old Emerald Isle.

LAWYERS

EVERY LAWYER IN AMERICA would be a lot more trustworthy if he was forced to go straight from his bar exam to the penitentiary for five years. Which is where he would share a cell with Leroy Washington Jefferson or Moose Deliverance, as Sidewall says, and have to answer that immediate question of whether he wants to be the wife or the husband.

On those occasions when Bubba has a legal problem, he likes to go with the strength. Shoot for a probable win and guarantee yourself no worse than a tie.

That's why he always turns the matter over to Glickstein, Weinreb, Weinberg, Rosen & Siegel.

Their names alone strike fear in the other side.

JUDGES

BUBBA HAS NEVER FIGURED OUT why, exactly, but it always seems to be the fellow known around town as "The Hanging Judge" who gets exposed in the newspaper one day for being the proud owner of an enviable pornography collection.

JOGGERS

BUBBA BELIEVES THAT JOGGERS have as much right to kill themselves as any other group, but he would like to see more of them doing it in places outside of the United States.

They wouldn't particularly bother anybody in the Amazon, for instance, and it would do wonders for the traffic congestion in American cities.

It is Bubba's observation that joggers are among the people who complain the most about "passive" cigarette smoke. He would therefore like to file a complaint about the "passive" body odor that joggers inflict on civilization.

He frequently asks friends: Have you ever smelled a jogger on a street corner, or even a dead one in a city park?

YUPPIES

BUBBA NEVER DID LIKE TO LOOK at their wet hair and tennis shirts, but he doesn't think they seriously annoy anybody other than the people on the other end of their car phones.

"GAYS"

GAY WAS A PERFECTLY GOOD word in the English language, Bubba says, until a gang of San Francisco waiters stole it—they wanted a word that would make the things they do with one another sound festive.

Bubba doesn't think the general public buys it, even though a lot of dim-witted newspapers try to help it along.

Like Sidewall says, "Your perverts are either queers or lesbians, fags or dykes, limpos or hiking boots. If they're not ashamed of it, why don't they call themselves what they are?"

It's Joe Ed who says, "They're hopping out of the closet all the time, and for what? They already own Halloween and Mardi Gras. They've got a foothold there you couldn't bust loose with napalm."

For his part, Bubba can't understand why so many "gays" want to be in the armed forces of the United States. He guesses they don't realize their military comrades will be tempted to get rid of them and make it look like accidents.

One by one your "gay" service person will disappear off the deck of a ship, fall out of an airplane, or get picked up in a foxhole and thrown to a Serb.

Sidewall brought another perspective to the subject one evening at Dottie's.

He said if he had to choose between being a "gay" man or a "gay" woman, he'd rather be a dyke.

"With what you have to work with," he said, "it's bound to be more fun making love to a lesbian. It's common sense."

BISEXUALS

THIS IS A REAL PUZZLER FOR some people. But Sidewall Thornton probably summed it up when a young fellow in Sidewall's office thought he could confide in Sidewall about the sexual urges he was feeling for both women and men.

"Women *and* men?" Sidewall said. "That's a load of shit, Rodney. You either like to suck dicks or you don't."

PREACHERS

WHEN BUBBA WAS A LITTLE kid, he had his pants scared off by preachers. Didn't matter whether it was Dr. J. Frank Horner at his mama's church or Rev. L. N. Duckworth at his daddy's church.

They both assured Bubba he would burn in eternal hell if he ever stole another Butterfinger out of Mr. Goolsby's drugstore or rode his bicycle through Old Lady Foster's gladiolas again.

It wasn't until Bubba became an adult that he realized preachers were no different from anyone else, aside from being long-winded.

As Bubba remarked to the born-again Melissa one night in the midst of a religious discussion, "Well, tell me this. Why is it that, yea, though they walk through the valley of Hondas, they usually manage to drive off in Cadillacs?"

The born-again Melissa said Bubba was a heathen and heathens weren't funny and she would tell the Lord to put a curse on his goddamn ass.

Bubba then said he would wager that more than one preacher had visited a motel room with a lady other than Mrs. Preacher, and had said, "Let's see what happens if thy gets thineself down here on this rod or staff, whichever thy verily wants to call it."

That may have been the night Bubba had to dodge the clock radio. It was near the end with Old No. 3.

TEXAS

BUBBA   HAS   STUDIED   TEXANS closely through the years and he has come to a conclusion. You shouldn't scoff at your Texan for buying into all that Alamo bullshit. This is what gives your Texan confidence to deal with Easterners and all that pilgrim bullshit.

FLORIDA

BUBBA SAYS THERE IS A LOT more to Florida than hurricanes, Cubans, and alligators. It has more golf courses than any other state, everybody lives on some kind of inlet, and there's a hill to look at over near Ocala. He does admit, however, that you rarely see anything behind the wheel of a car but hats and knuckles.

CALIFORNIA

BUBBA HAD A BUDDY NAMED Harold who got a big promotion and was transferred out to California. It didn't take long for Harold to turn arrogant and start talking about sunsets and discussing wine and eating spinach salads.

Bubba hopes Harold was opening a nice Chablis for himself when the mudslide ran off with his living room and Porsche.

NEW YORK CITY

THE WAY TO HANDLE NEW YORK City, Bubba says, is never let on that you're intimidated or flustered.

To begin with, talking up there is easy. You never have to finish a sentence in Manhattan—somebody will do it for you.

You need to understand immediately that all those people who want to trample you to death on Fifth Avenue have a perfect right to do it. They live there and you don't.

If Guido gets shot and killed while he's standing next to you on a corner, act like everybody else. You didn't see it. Buy your hot dog and move on.

Never let a bartender know that you think forty-seven dollars is too much money for a couple of drinks. And be sure to tip twenty-five dollars so he will remember you when you come in again and won't charge you eighty-nine dollars for a couple of drinks.

Don't be a pest when you go in one of those restaurants where you've been told you'll see "celebrities." Let Kunta Kinte and Dan Rather have their dinner in peace.

Gladly give money to anybody on the street who asks for it. For instance, that homeless fellow in the doorway may have a .350 Magnum under his blanket with the pepperoni pizza.

Sometimes, you might be inclined to give extra money for originality.

That's what Bubba did when the little dude came up to him near the skating rink in Rockefeller Center and asked if Bubba wanted to contribute to "U.N.S.F.—the United Negro Sandwich Fund."

RUSSIA

I T'S NO BIG SURPRISE TO BUBBA that communism and dry cleaning and a lot of other things don't work in Russia. Russians still haven't noticed after all this time that half the letters in their alphabet are backward.

CHINA

SMALL WONDER YOUR CHINAMEN are inscrutable, Bubba says. They talk in pictures.

If you could understand it, you would know that Fu Wong is saying to his wife, Ching Ling, "Honey, let's get dressed up tonight in our oblong boxes with slanty slashes and go eat some of those triangles with curlicues we like over at the leaning rectangle with the dipping roof. We better drive your Doodle. My Hieroglyphic is low on gas."

ARABS

IT DOESN'T MATTER WHAT COUN-
try they're from, Bubba says, your Arabs are all
the same people, even when they happen to be
Persians—and you're never going to be able to understand or comprehend a raghead sumbitch who
sleeps with his eyes open and a knife in his teeth
and killed his own brother three days ago.

How to deal with Arabs seems to be a question that frustrates a lot of governments, but it's no
great dilemma for Bubba.

Take away their goats. They can't last all
that long on bug-kabob.

COLLEGES

WHEN BUBBA WAS IN COL-
lege for a while, they were just starting
to teach revolution and socialism, but
he missed out on those courses—they always
seemed to conflict with football practice or his gin
rummy lab.

Bubba has no idea what they tried to teach
Bubba Junior and Janie Junior. They went to a big
state university where they turn you into a Social
Security number and put you in a classroom with
five hundred other Social Security numbers.

In a situation like that, Bubba doubts that
Janie Junior would have learned much, even if she
hadn't been knocked up and had to drop out. She
seems happy enough today, married to Darrell, the
part-time sheetrocker and full-time arms merchant.

Bubba Junior somehow managed to gradu-
ate after five and a half years and find a job as a
salesman, a chip off the old Bubba. His daddy
thinks he'll do all right, too, as soon as he learns to
get along better with those pricks he's working for.

LIBERALS

LIBERALS DESERVE ALL THE SYM-
pathy they can get, Bubba says, because of
the constant disappointments and inconve-
niences they suffer.

Their Lincoln Town Cars are too big to fit in
most parking spaces.

They can't ever seem to find housekeepers
who make them completely happy.

The beaches are eroding in front of their second homes.

Private school tuitions are always going up.

Right in front of them, people who aren't liberals have the audacity to practice free speech.

Every time they elect a migrant worker to
public office, what happens? The first thing he does
is join a country club and take up golf.

It's just one heartbreak after another for liberals, but Bubba thinks you have to admire their
stamina.

CONSERVATIVES

ONSERVATIVES NEED SYMPATHY just as much as liberals, Bubba observes, but for a different set of reasons.

1. General Douglas MacArthur is still dead.
2. They've never had their own network news anchor.
3. An increasing number of people they've never heard of are getting rich.
4. More and more people keep taking it the wrong way when a conservative says, "A little ethnic cleansing never hurt anything."
5. Far too many oddball groups, such as Republicans and Democrats, are claiming the American flag belongs to them, too.

ORGANIZATIONS

EXCEPT FOR BOOSTER CLUBS that buy sports cars and three-bedroom apartments for college football recruits, Bubba thinks most organizations are silly.

The silliest ones always seem to be the loudest and most energetic, he's noticed.

A few he has come across lately:

Society for the Prevention of Smoking in Your Own Home and Automobile.

Coalition Against Discrimination in Anything We Might Happen to Think of Next.

Screamers for a Quieter Earth.

Citizens Opposed to Laughter in Public Buildings.

Pro Life for the Death Penalty.

We Are Right and You Are Wrong About Everything So You Better Agree with Us or It's Going to Get Pretty Noisy Around the Workplace.

RICH PEOPLE

BASICALLY, THERE ARE TWO kinds. There are those who inherit money and there are those who make it themselves. Bubba hears it said that there's a third category—the person who inherits wealth, then makes a lot more money with it—but he says this is the same thing as recovering a fumble on the other team's four-yard line, wind at your back.

People who inherit money tend to have good manners and act polite all the time, even though Harvard hasn't had a good football team since 1931. At the same time, they have this somewhat irritating habit of never going anywhere near their pocket when the dinner check comes.

People who start from scratch and make their own fortunes, on the other hand, don't seem to be afraid to spend it. They go out and buy all the toys, travel around, live on islands part of the time, and enjoy life to the fullest—right up to the day they're indicted.

FAKE RICH PEOPLE

FAKE RICH PEOPLE LIVE IN TRACT mansions behind security gates on streets named for the Seven Dwarfs, Indian tribes, and Scottish golf courses.

"We're at 52933 Dopey Lane just off Blackfoot Drive near Old Troon Circle. Call before you come and we'll leave your name with the guard at the south entrance—and don't forget to bring your swimsuit, tennis racket, baseball glove, archery bow, fly rod, and putter."

Bubba is never surprised to discover that the husbands in this enchanted neighborhood frequently wear more jewelry than the wives.

Well, by golly, those fellows deserve to decorate themselves for selling all those R.V.s.

Bubba hears that all of his ex-wives have found peace and contentment in this paradise, working on the snack bar committee, collecting clothes, taking their power walks, chatting with their friends about whether it's too hot or too cold.

He wishes Janie Ruth and Vicki Lynn and Melissa cheerful brunches for the rest of their lives and hopes that their credit cards don't come upon more trouble than a run-over dog.

Every so often, Bubba sees one of the happy couples in the mall. Everybody will nod politely.

It's usually on a night when Bubba and Priscilla Ann are on the way to Cinema 12, an evening when Priscilla Ann is in the mood for what she calls "one of those dialogue movies."

THE FAT LADY

WHEN IS IT OVER? THAT WAS the major discussion at Dottie's Paradise Lounge the other night.

Joe Ed Starkey said it's not over till the fat lady approves your loan.

Sidewall Thornton said it's not over till the fat lady stops paying workers' comp to all those bums.

Bubba said it's not over till the fat lady winds up your tax audit.

A despondent stranger at the bar said it's not over till the fat lady gives you the zoning clearance.

Joe Ed said, "I suppose it's almost over if the fat lady is your wife."

Sidewall said, "It's probably over if that fat lady who's singing is your nurse."

Bubba said, "I don't think we need to worry about it anytime soon. It can't possibly be over till the fat lady gets off the green."

ABOUT THE AUTHOR

DAN JENKINS HAS WRITTEN many other books that he can remember better than the books other people have written. Among them are the best-selling novels *Semi-Tough, Dead Solid Perfect, Baja Oklahoma, Life Its Ownself,* and *You Gotta Play Hurt.*

He occasionally writes movies, for money. Every decade or so, one of them even makes it to the screen.

A native of Fort Worth, Texas, he now lives in Ponte Vedra Beach, Florida, with his lovely wife, June, who has been forgiving his typewriter for three decades now, and their Yorkshire terrier, Barbara Jane, a spoiled, flirtatious, self-absorbed debutante who summers in Switzerland and would be the last to know she's a dog.

For twenty-three years, Jenkins regularly provoked the readers of *Sports Illustrated.* He now provokes the readers of *Golf Digest* with a monthly column and essays on major events.

He has never had a real job.

Jenkins has studied Bubba for over forty years. He confesses to being about one-third Bubba himself.

His journalist daughter, Sally, and his two photographer sons, Marty and Danny, say it's more like two-thirds.